LAND OF THE FREE

The Statue of Liberty

Anne Hempstead

Heinemann Library
Chicago, Illinois

For more information address the publisher:
Raintree, 100 N. LaSalle, Suite 1200, Chicago IL 60602

Printed in China by WKT Company Limited

10 09 08 07 06
10 9 8 7 6 5 4 3 2 1

ISBN 1-4034-7004-9 (hc) -- ISBN 1-4034-7011-1 (pb)

Library of Congress Cataloging-in-Publication Data:
Cataloging-in-publication data is on file at the Library of Congress.

Photo Research: Julie Laffin

Acknowledgments
The author and publisher are grateful to the following for permission to reproduce copyright material:
p.4 Corbis, pp.6,8, 12, 22, 24 Corbis/Bettmann, pp.10, 14, 17, 18, 21 Library of Congress, p.27 Corbis/Peter Trunley

Cover photo: Corbis/Zefa/Alan Schein

The paper used to print this book comes from sustainable resources.

Contents

Chapter One:
A Grand Idea

For many people all over the world, the Statue of Liberty is a **symbol** of freedom and of the United States. But the idea for the Statue of Liberty did not begin in the United States. It began as a casual remark about freedom and friendship made at a dinner party in France in 1865.

A group gathered at a home of Edouard de Laboulaye outside Paris, France, to discuss politics. At the time, Emperor Napoleon III ruled France. The emperor ruled France in a way that took away many of the rights of French citizens.

Laboulaye was a prominent law professor and member of the French Senate. He admired the United States for its principles of individual freedom and **democracy**. De Laboulaye and his guests fiercely opposed France's current government.

At the party, the guests talked about the friendship between France and the United States. During the Revolutionary War, France had provided weapons, soldiers, and money to the North American colonies.

Frenchmen like the Marquis de Lafayette had served in the army. After independence, George Washington chose the French engineer Pierre L'Enfant to plan the new nation's capitol, Washington, D.C.

The guests wanted to build a new French **republic** using American **democracy** as their model. De Laboulaye had an idea. The United States was approaching its 100-year anniversary. To celebrate, de Laboulaye proposed that France give the American people a great **monument** in honor of human liberty. Such a gift would cement the friendship between the two countries. He also believed it would help to win American support for the struggle for self-government in France.

Frédéric Auguste Bartholdi

De Laboulaye's suggestion immediately captured the imagination of one of the guests, a young **sculptor** named Frédéric Auguste Bartholdi. Bartholdi had studied painting, architecture, and sculpture as a student in Paris. At the age of 19, he had created a larger-than-life statue of French hero

Frédéric Auguste Bartholdi, the sculptor of the Statue of Liberty.

Neoclassical style

In art and architecture, the term *neoclassical* refers to work that draws upon details from Greek and Roman designs. This style was very popular during the American and French revolutions. The revolutionaries saw the Greeks and Romans as being examples of early democracies. The style became less popular in the early nineteenth century, but continues to be used today.

General Jean Rapp. Measuring 12 feet (4 meters) in height, the statue almost touched the ceiling in the artist's studio. The statue was a huge success.

De Laboulaye's suggestion for a monument especially appealed to Bartholdi. He had developed a passion for large monuments. Such a great statue would test his artist talent. It would also give him the chance to express his belief in freedom and democracy. Looking back years later, Bartholdi wrote that the idea for the monument became deeply "fixed" in his mind. For the next twenty-one years, Bartholdi worked to make the monument to liberty a reality.

Art on a grand scale

Bartholdi was not alone in his love of grand art. Large-scale public monuments and freestanding statues became very popular in the nineteenth century. Statues and monuments were created to honor heroic military or political leaders, to remember important political events, or to symbolize principles and ideals. Like many other artists of his time, Bartholdi traveled to Egypt to study the wonders of the ancient world. The young sculptor was overwhelmed by the size and magnificence of the Pyramids and the Great Sphinx. He returned to France determined to make something of **colossal** size.

In 1867 Bartholdi drew up plans for a lighthouse for the Suez Canal. He proposed a dramatic concept based upon classical Roman statues and the Colossus of Rhodes. Bartholdi's lighthouse was in the form of a giant Egyptian woman holding a torch. He called his lighthouse "Egypt Bringing the Light to Asia." The lighthouse was never built, but the idea of the woman and the torch stayed in Bartholdi's imagination.

Bartholdi was convinced it was time to create a statue honoring American liberty. A war between France and Germany had brought the downfall of Napoleon III, and France was ready for a political change. De Laboulaye encouraged Bartholdi to go to America. He hoped the idea

The Colossus of Rhodes

The Colossus of Rhodes was one of the seven wonders of the ancient world. It is believed to have been a giant 150-foot-high (46-meter-high) bronze statue of Helios, the god of the sun. The Statue overlooked the harbor of the Greek island of Rhodes for 56 years before an earthquake caused it to crumble.

for the statue would help his efforts to create a French **Republic**. Bartholdi agreed, even though he had not yet decided what form the statue would take. In 1871 Bartholdi traveled to the United States to raise support for his cause.

Before he set foot on U.S. soil, Bartholdi found the perfect place for his statue. Standing on the deck as his ship sailed into New York Harbor, Bartholdi saw a small island in the Hudson River. He now had his vision for the statue. Bartholdi imagined a **colossal** sculpture of a woman with a torch standing on the island. He saw future travelers to the United States being welcomed by his statue. It would be their thrilling first view of the New World.

Over the next few months, Bartholdi traveled around the United States showing a sketch of the statue and promoting the project. Many people were supportive of the idea, but no one was willing to donate money to the cause.

He returned home empty-handed, but the French still wanted to build the statue. The statue was estimated to cost $250,000. De Laboulaye formed the Union Franco-American with members from both nations. They decided to share the expenses. France would pay for the statue, and America would pay for the **pedestal**. Money slowly started to come in, with many donations coming from French children.

Bartholdi developed several small clay models showing the statue in different poses. The final model was unveiled on November 6, 1875, at a formal dinner held by the Union. The model won over several wealthy families including the Lafayettes, who then contributed larger amounts of money to the cause. At last, Bartholdi was able to begin work on the statue.

Chapter Two:
Freedom Becomes a Statue

Bartholdi made a plaster model to show his carpenters, copper workers, and other workers how to build the **monument**. To calculate the dimensions, or full-scale measurements, for the 151-foot [46-meter] statue, the first model was doubled to make a second model that was 9 feet [3 meters] high. This model's dimensions were enlarged 4 times to make a 38-foot [11-meter] model. This model was divided into parts, each of which was enlarged four times to get the final dimensions. Then work began on what would become the statue's hands.

As the project progressed, larger models were built. Lines and surfaces were measured based on a set of points marked on the models and connected with strips of wood. The wood was later covered with plaster to create the models for the copper covering.

Bartholdi chose copper for the giant figure because it was lighter and less expensive than bronze or stone. But it would have to hold up to the salt air and high winds in New York Harbor.

Every detail in the statue helps to convey ideas about liberty:

- The torch (A) represents the light of knowledge and reason that leads to freedom. The Statue's original name is "Liberty Enlightening the World."

- The seven spikes of the crown (B) represent the seven seas and seven continents.

- Liberty holds in her left hand a tablet (C) representing the Book of Law. The tablet is in the shape of a keystone. In architecture, a keystone is a stone placed in the center of an arch. It keeps the stones in place and the arch from collapsing. Bartholdi used the keystone tablet to symbolize the idea that laws bring stability to **democratic** government.

- The Roman numeral inscription July IV MDCCLXXVI (D) means "July 4, 1776," America's date of independence.

- Liberty is dressed in the tradition of the Roman goddess Libertas. She wears a cloak called a palla over a draped robe, or stola (E).

- On her feet she wears sandals (F), a symbol of a free person. Liberty's right foot is raised, making her appear to be walking from the broken chains or shackles (G) at her feet. Bartholdi gave her this pose to suggest that she carries her torch to light the path to freedom. The chains at Liberty's feet can only be seen from the torch or the air above her.

There was also another factor to consider: the statue would be hollow inside. The artist needed the help of an engineer to ensure that the statue would be stable. He asked Alexandre-Gustave Eiffel to design the inside **armature** for the statue. This would be the "skeleton" that would support the copper "skin" of the statue.

Eiffel's design for the **armature** was very inventive. Down the center of the statue, he placed an iron **pylon** made from four iron beams bolted with cross braces. A secondary framework was attached to the pylon. This was the statue's skeleton. Then sheets of thin copper—the "skin"— were connected to the framework by a set of short bars. This framework of interconnected iron beams gave the statue strength and flexibility.

Because the statue was so large, the copper had to be formed in parts, or segments. Pre-cut pieces of copper were pressed and hammered by hand against the inside of molds, or casts, to create a finished image on the outside surface. This method is called *repousse*.

Symbolism in the Statue of Liberty

Bartholdi wanted the Statue of Liberty to be a **symbol** of the desire in all people to be free. He created a female figure in the style of a Roman goddess to represent the universal ideal of freedom. Bartholdi may have modeled the statue's face after his mother's.

The torch comes home

Twenty men worked twelve hours a day on the statue, but time ran out. It would not be ready in time for the 1876 American Centennial Exhibition in Philadelphia, Pennsylvania. So Bartholdi sent the statue's arm and torch as a taste of what was to come. The Americans were not disappointed. Hundreds of visitors walked inside the arm and climbed a narrow ladder to the torch, where they viewed the exhibition fairgrounds.

The arm and torch created enthusiasm for the project. In December 1876 the American Committee was organized to raise funds for the statue's **pedestal**. On February 22, 1877, Congress authorized the government to accept the statue and provide a site for it, as well as provide funds for its maintenance.

Meanwhile work on the statue continued. The statue's head and shoulders were finished in time for the Paris International Exposition of 1878. Crowds cheered as Liberty was pulled through the streets of Paris on a cart drawn by

Liberty's head was displayed in Paris in 1878.

~ 14 ~

thirteen horses. By July 1882, the top half of the statue was complete. In December Bartholdi informed the American Committee that the statue was reaching above the houses and by spring would overlook Paris itself.

America builds the pedestal

The statue was nearing completion, but the American Committee had not made any effort to finance its share of the project—building the pedestal. Finally, in January 1882, the committee published an appeal for money in newspapers across the United States. Everyone from individual citizens to Chambers of Commerce, trade groups, social clubs, and student organizations was asked to contribute. The American people, however, did not eagerly open their wallets. Less than $85,000 was collected. To make matters worse, Congress voted down a bill that would set aside $100,000 for the building of the pedestal.

Despite these setbacks, Richard Morris Hunt, one of America's most popular architects, drew up plans for the pedestal. In April 1883, workmen began to work on the foundation.

The concrete and granite pedestal was a feat in its own right. It was nicknamed the "Grand Footstool of Liberty." Like the statue, it has huge proportions, or measurements. The pedestal towers 89 feet [27 meters] high and has 20-foot [6-meter] thick concrete walls. It sits on a huge pyramid-shaped foundation. At the time it was built, the foundation was the largest single concrete mass ever poured. The pedestal is so large that today it houses a museum.

Pulitzer saves the statue

By March 1885, the statue was completed in Paris and ready to ship to the United States, but work on the pedestal had stopped. Although $180,000 had been collected, the cost of the **pedestal** had doubled over its first estimate. The Statue of Liberty, as it had come to be popularly known, arrived in New York packed in 214 crates and waited for her pedestal.

Joseph Pulitzer, a newspaper publisher, decided to lead a fundraising effort. Part of his reason for doing so was to increase sales of his newspaper. In May 1883 his paper, *The World*, had run an editorial scolding the wealthy people who had failed to contribute to the project. The campaign was unsuccessful; but in March 1885, Pulitzer renewed his drive. This time he ran his editorial on the front page every day for six months. Now the public responded to Pulitzer's appeal with great enthusiasm. Pulitzer published the name of everyone who sent in a donation, no matter how small. Over 120,000 Americans donated, for a total of $100,000.

The pedestal was completed on April 22, 1886. To celebrate, workers threw handfuls of silver coins into the wet mortar before setting the last granite block. A bronze box was buried placed inside the cornerstone. The box contained newspapers of the day, a history of the statue, information about the Declaration of Independence, and an 1864 fifty-cent silver coin.

Liberty unveiled

On October 28, 1886, a crowd of people gathered on Bedloe's Island to **dedicate** the Statue of Liberty. The group included members of the French and American committees, city officials, policeman, cadets, students, bands, President Grover Cleveland, and Frédéric Auguste Bartholdi. The official speechmakers stood on a platform erected next to

Liberty is partially obscured by smoke from the canons during her unveiling ceremony.

the statue. Bartholdi climbed up to the statue's crown. He had the honor of pulling the cord that would remove the French flag covering the statue's face.

Bartholdi was too far away to hear the speakers. A boy in stationed near the platform was supposed to signal him when William Evarts, the head of the American Committee finished talking. When the boy gave the signal Bartholdi pulled the cord unveiling the statue's face. Cannons fired, whistles blew, and the crowd roared its approval.

Chapter Three: Mother of Exiles

Bartholdi created his statue as a gift of friendship and as a **symbol** of freedom. Over time, in the course of events in American history, the statue took on an additional meaning.

In the late 1800s and early 1900s, European **immigrants** entered the United States in record numbers. Men, women, and children came to America in search of a better life. Their home countries were troubled with war, persecution, famine, and poverty. America was seen as the land of opportunity. For thousands, as Bartholdi predicted, their first view of the New World was the Statue of Liberty as they sailed into New York Harbor.

Ellis Island and immigration

In 1808 the state of New York sold Ellis Island to the U.S. government. During the Revolutionary War, the British had been able to sail into New York Harbor with no trouble.

After the revolution, the government realized that it needed some defense in the harbor. The fortifications built on Ellis Island helped defend the country from the British during the war of 1812. The island was named after New York merchant Samuel Ellis, who once owned the island. For a long time shipping waste was dumped at the island, and much of the island's 27-acre (11-hectare) current area is a landfill.

Before 1890, individual states had handled immigration into the country. In 1892, six years after Liberty's dedication, nearby Ellis Island became the official entry station for immigration. Over 12 million **immigrants** were admitted to the United States through Ellis Island. It is believed that nearly 40 percent of all Americans living today can trace their ancestry to back to one of those 12 million. Annie Moore, a fifteen-year-old Irish girl was the first immigrant to come through Ellis Island.

First and second-class passengers were processed on the ships on which they arrived. It was assumed that anyone who could afford a first-class ticket would not become a burden to his or her new country. Passengers who traveled in lower-priced third or steerage classes were taken to Ellis Island for medical and legal examinations. About two percent of the immigrants were denied entry. Most of these were denied entry for medical reasons, such as if the doctors believed the person had a disease that might spread to other people.

Immigrants to the U.S. having their eyes inspected as part of a medical exam at Ellis Island.

In 1897 a fire burned the immigration station to the ground. Some immigration records dating back to 1855 were destroyed in the fire. On December 17, 1900, a new fireproof building was built and 2,251 immigrants were processed that day.

Immigrants continued to pour into Ellis Island until 1924, after which its role was reduced. In 1943 most immigration processing was done in New York City itself. In 1956 the immigration station on Ellis Island was closed. The buildings began to fall into disrepair. In 1965 Ellis Island became part of the Statue of Liberty National Monument. Private citizens raised money to restore the island, and the Island's main building was reopened in 1990 as a museum.

Many of the immigrants who entered the United States through Ellis Island were fleeing poverty, religious persecution, and political unrest. It was fitting that their first site of their new country was Lady Liberty.

Emma Lazarus

On November 2, 1883, Emma Lazarus wrote a poem for a fundraising event. The sonnet was intended to raise money for the Bartholdi **pedestal** fund.

Lazarus wrote about the Statue of Liberty. Although she was the daughter of a wealthy man, Lazarus had worked among New York's poorest Russian **immigrants**. In her poem, Lazarus captured the immigrants' need for freedom and protection.

She compared the Statue of Liberty to the Colossus of Rhodes. But unlike the bold conqueror, the Statue of Liberty was a mild-eyed mother welcoming the poor people of the world to her land of freedom. The poem added new meaning to the statue. The Statue was now a **symbol** of hope for a new life free from **oppression**. In 1903 the words to the poem were carved onto a plaque that was placed on a wall of the pedestal.

Preserving Liberty

At first, management of the statue was the responsibility of the

Poet Emma Lazarus is best known for the poem "The New Colossus," which is on a plaque on the pedestal of the Statue of Liberty.

The New Colossus

Not like the brazen giant of Greek fame,
With conquering limbs astride from land to land;
Here at our sea-washed, sunset gates shall stand
A mighty woman with a torch, whose flame
Is the imprisoned lightning, and her name
Mother of Exiles. From her beacon-hand
Glows world-wide welcome; her mild eyes command
The air-bridged harbor that twin cities frame.
"Keep ancient lands, your storied pomp!" cries she
With silent lips. "Give me your tired, your poor,
Your huddled masses yearning to breathe free,
The wretched refuse of your teeming shore.
Send these, the homeless, tempest-tost to me,
I lift my lamp beside the golden door!"

lighthouse board. It was thought that the statue might double as a lighthouse. However, the statue's torch did not give off enough light. In 1901, management was turned over to the U.S. War Department.

The American Committee helped establish the statue's tourist business. It began a ferry service to continue raising money for the statue's maintenance. Crowds of visitors arrived on the island. Visitors loved to climb the winding staircases to reach the observation windows in the torch and the crown. Eventually structural problems and narrow passageways made the arm unsafe, and the torch was closed to visitors in 1916. The Statue was declared a national monument by President Calvin Coolidge on October 15, 1924, and placed in the care of the National Park Service in 1933. In 1956 Bedloe's Island was renamed Liberty Island.

Chapter Four:
Liberty Today

In 1986 Liberty celebrated her 100th, or centennial, birthday. The statue was clearly showing her age. Weather, pollution, and foot traffic had left her in need of many expensive repairs. In 1982 fund-raising efforts to finance the project began. The response of the American people was dramatic. They gave more than $500 million to restore, preserve, and maintain the Statue and Ellis Island.

An army of architects, engineers, and historians tackled the project. The first problem facing the architects was that Bartholdi and Eiffel had left no detailed drawings that showed how they had designed and built the Statue. French and American research teams used old photos, notes, sketches, letters and thousands of measurements to create a complete set of architectural and engineering plans. The drawings were used to make computer models.

People worried that cleaning the exterior of the statue would remove the wonderful **patina** that gives the statue its green color. The team used modern preservation and restoration guidelines and methods. Every effort was made to preserve the patina, because it protects the metal from corroding, or wearing away. Then the exterior was power washed to remove stains and bird droppings.

Other restoration efforts included removing rust and corrosion, replacing the **armature** and rivets, mending tears on the nose, eyes, lips, and chin, replacing a missing hair curl, and repairing the shackles. The team discovered that the arm and torch were out of alignment. Finally the torch, which had been redesigned, was restored to Bartholdi's original plan. The statue was **dedicated** in its renewed form on October 28, 1986.

Eternal symbol

Today the Statue of Liberty is as popular as ever. Thousands of tourists take ferries from Manhattan and New Jersey to visit the Statue. Shortly after the terrorist attacks of September 11, 2001, the Park Service briefly closed the Statue. Today, much of the statue and its grounds are once again open to visitors.

The image of the Statue is known worldwide. It has been used on everything from advertisements to wartime enlistment posters. Lady Liberty has even appeared in movies. Perhaps her most famous role was in the *Planet of the Apes*. At the end of the movie, she appears on a desolate beach half buried. Her presence shows that the planet of the apes is actually Earth.

There have been many replicas, or copies, made of the statue. In France, a smaller copy stands in Paris on an island in the Seine River. There is a copy in Bartholdi's hometown of Colmar, and another in Bordeaux. For 100 years, a 37-foot (11-meter) replica stood on top of the Liberty Warehouse in Manhattan.

The replica is now part of the Brooklyn Museum of Art collection.

On May 30, 1989, the world saw a new Goddess of Liberty. Students in China made a 28-foot-high (10-meter-high) Styrofoam and plaster statue of a young woman holding a torch in both hands. The students raised their statue in Tiananmen Square to show their support for the **Democracy** movement in China. The Goddess of Liberty stood for five days before army tanks tore it down. The protest ended in violence, but the image of the Chinese Goddess of Freedom was broadcast around the world. The Statue of Liberty continues to be a **symbol** inspiring a universal hope for freedom and democracy.

Protesters in Tiananmen Square, China display their own Liberty Statue.

Timeline

1865 American Civil War ends. Idea for statue is born as at Laboulaye's dinner party in France.

1871 Bartholdi comes to America

1876 The torch arm is exhibited in Philadelphia

1877 Congress accepts Liberty as a gift from France

1878 Liberty head is displayed in Paris

1881 Hunt begins designing **pedestal**

1884 Statue construction completed in Paris

1885 Liberty is taken apart and shipped to America. Pulitzer campaign helps to complete the pedestal

1886 The pedestal is completed. Statue is reassembled. "Liberty Enlightening the World" is dedicated on October 28

1924 Statue of Liberty is declared a national **monument**

1956 Bedloe's Island renamed Liberty Island

1986 Restoration is completed on 100-year-old Statue. Liberty celebrates her centennial on July 4 and is officially rededicated on October 28

Further Information

Interesting facts about the Statue of Liberty

- In winds of 50 miles (80 kilometers) per hour or more, the Statue of Liberty will sway 3 inches (8 centimeters) to either side. The torch will sway 5 inches (13 centimeters).

- A single fingernail on the statue weighs about 3.5 pounds (1.5 kilograms).

- The total weight of the Statue of Liberty is 450,000 pounds (225 tons).

- As fabric, the Statue of Liberty's dress would measure approximately 4,000 square yards (3,658 square meters).

- Each of the Statue of Liberty's feet is 25 feet (8 meters) long. In American shoe sizes, she would wear a size 879!

The Statue of Liberty National Monument is open to visitors every day except December 25th. To learn more about how to visit the Statue, go to: www.nps.gov/stli/

Further Reading

Hochain, Serge. *Building Liberty: A Statue Is Born.* Washington, D.C.: National Geographic Press, 2004.

Glossary

armature framework used by a sculptor to support a model

colossal very large

dedicate set something apart for an important purpose

democracy government in which the people hold the power

immigrant person who moves to a new country

monument statue or building created to honor a person, group, or event

oppression to keep down by harsh and unfair treatment

patina green film that forms on copper after it has been exposed to the air for a long time

pedestal base of a statue

pylon tower-like structure

republic government with a chief of state such as a president

sculptor artist who creates structures or statues

symbol something that stands for something else

Index